Mr Deputy Vice-Chancellor, Ladies and Gentlemen,

In 1724, the elector of Hanover, engaged as king of England in founding a monarchic dynasty, endowed a chair of modern history at the University of Cambridge. (Also at Oxford, of course, but that is not this day a matter of major concern.) In 1808, one Samuel Meyer Ehrenberg, engaged (though he did not know it) in founding a modest scholarly dynasty, took over an ailing school at Wolfenbüttel, a few miles from Hanover though then in the neighbouring duchy of Brunswick. In 1983, a descendant of the former bestowed her ancestor's foundation upon a descendant of the latter, thus keeping things within the old territorial relations. Indeed, the connexion was symbolized even more clearly. The elector of Hanover and the duke of Brunswick, both being Guelphs, were in a manner of speaking cousins; and in 1983 the holders of both those Regius chairs at Oxford and Cambridge are cousins too. There is a certain satisfactory rotundity about these essentially improbable events.

When I look back upon the history of the chair which now I have the great honour to occupy, I find myself even more impressed than usual by the mysterious ways of providence, or rather, perhaps, by the unpredictability of human purposes manifestly not controlled by providence. For about a century and a half the existence of Regius professors of modern history in this University could easily have escaped notice, though a few of them gave lectures. The chair was in fact precisely 151 years old

I

when at last the academic claims of history found recognition here, by the inappropriate but normal device of turning it into a tripos of its own. The achievement belonged to the first truly notable Regius professor, Sir John Seeley, who, by the way, died in office one year younger in age than is the present occupant upon taking up his duties. Seeley had succeeded to Charles Kingsley, the last of the absurdities, and his inaugural lecture provided the occasion for the finest double anti-compliment ever uttered: a story so familiar that I will not repeat it here. I have good reason to feel that this time, too, an inaugural lecture will induce regrets for the departure of my predecessor, but on this occasion there will be no implication adverse to the retired tenant. To succeed to Owen Chadwick is both an honour and a burden. How can one possibly expect to emulate one who rather gave distinction to the chair than derived distinction from it? He will, I think, prove to have been the last honestly qualified Regius professor of modern history, for the modern history of King George's devising is all history since the fall of Rome. And here we had a man who took all modern history as his province, giving it lustre wherever he touched it. The *Times* newspaper has already inadvertently extended his tenure into mine, and quite right too. While he lives, Owen will remain *the* Regius professor: I and my successors will always acknowledge his primacy.

Since 1875, history and its professor, soon joined by other persons of the same standing though never by a professor of English history until Sir John Plumb and I wrote the mark of chauvinism into our temporary titles, have increasingly flourished in this University. Nor was this only – though until the English tripos rose to prominence this was often the case – because history provided a refuge for those undergraduates who had to pretend to read something if they were to be admitted at all. History and its professors did indeed offer this service to a University anxious to attract fee-paying members – a service of which, to judge by some of the things I have heard said, an echo is still to be found in the M.Phil. in international studies spawned by the History Faculty. However, the Faculty and the University increasingly promoted the real thing too. The greatest of our historians, alas, was never Regius professor or indeed a member of the History Faculty: F. W. Maitland always disguised himself, not too successfully, as a lawyer. But the descent from Seeley testifies to the effect that a laying-on of hands will have, even though now and again (and I am told that this happens also in the Church) the hands alit upon somewhat surprising heads. Lord Acton, J. B. Bury, G. M. Trevelyan, G. N. Clark, J. R. M. Butler, David Knowles, Herbert Butterfield, Owen Chadwick: four knights, three heads of Houses, two O.M.s, one lord leaping – and one exclaustrated Benedictine. To write G. R. Elton after that does strike a discordant note of bathos. Ah well: a chair that survived such an inaugural address as Acton's, prescribing a regime which he had never succeeded in carrying out himself, should have no difficulty in surviving mine: some sort of consolation for the future.

What purpose did King George have in mind when in pudding-time he came over to introduce the University of Cambridge to the existence of a history that was neither Graeco-Roman nor, as they called it, ethnic? (There is a term of confusion for you: the present propagandists for ethnic history should know that they are really advocating

3

a study of the begats of the Old Testament.) Though Cambridge was unaware, England knew about it all right – an England which had produced William Camden, John Selden, Henry Spelman, Humphrey Wanley, Thomas Madox – and only the Universities needed to be apprised of the fact. The King made his purpose plain. It had come to his notice that the English Universities neglected precisely those studies which were needed to train servants of the state, particularly diplomats, who all needed to know modern history and foreign languages, the teaching of the latter being committed to lecturers which the professors were to pay out of their £40 stipends. (No such lecturers, not surprisingly, seem ever to have been appointed.) People, said the royal critic, wanting to acquire those useful skills were forced to rely on foreign tutors, a sad state of affairs. He intended his foundation to remedy these defects and thereby give academic institutions immersed in the study of the ancients a chance to contribute to current concerns. In accepting his gift, Cambridge looked forward to the time when 'a familiarity with the living tongues should be superadded to the dead ones . . . and when the appearance of an English gentleman in the courts of Europe with a governor of his own nation would not be so rare and uncommon as it theretofore had been'. (For the early history of the Regius chair I refer myself to Maitland's introduction to a collection entitled *Essays on the Teaching of History*, published by the University Press in 1901. The essays show how little has changed in either ambitions or achievements in eighty years.)

In reality, the King wanted more than native tutors for young noblemen doing the Grand Tour. He was not the last man to compare the English Universities with those of his own country, to the detriment of Oxford and Cambridge. At home he was used to Universities that concentrated on training the people the state relied on for the staffing of its services – theologians to run the state-dominated territorial churches, and jurists to run the secular administrations. In England he found institutions that consistently neglected the needs of government, producing clergy who no longer served the state and lightly polished gentlemen who with luck could read Horace on sight. So he set up professors of modern history and hoped for lecturers in languages. In return – what else do we expect? – he received words of praise which spoke well of those lecturers that were never set to the task and which altogether neglected to mention the professors of modern history. Still, it is quite a thought that this chair was founded for much the same reasons as those that today cause governments and social reformers to intrude upon our academic concerns.

As academic developments go, the 150 years that elapsed before King George I's real purpose was picked up and given some reality are not a terribly long time. Seeley also wished to use history to train governors of the realm, and from his tenure onwards Cambridge came increasingly to view the teaching of history in that light. Gradually history graduates overtook classicists as the mainstay of the civil service, and some of them joined a knowledge of French or even German to the wisdom they had gained from reading Stubbs. Until a generation ago one quite regularly encountered the opinion that the only respectable modern history to read – the only one that stretched the mind – was medieval; we have in our own day heard impassioned claims for the exclusive virtue of studies that terminate before the Reformation. I do not mean to decry medieval history – far from it. In particular I do not wish to give praise to really modern history, at a time when the history of the last hundred years in turn threatens to lay claim to being the only respectable form of modern history. I am anxious to remember that the chair I now hold pertains to all history since the fifth century, a fact which imposes a vast and unaccustomed tolerance upon its occupant. What has at times troubled me are the effects of overpraising the middle ages: such attitudes have before this prevented other bits of history from acquiring the right foundations of learning because medievalists have degraded them to an inbuilt inferiority.

However, such things, I hope, are in the past, as unhappily also is the notion that the study of modern history should be associated with the learning of foreign languages. There are still Universities in this country which demand a knowledge of French or German and so forth from any undergraduates who wish to study history, but Cambridge no longer belongs to that oldfangled group. When in order to accommodate our scientists we by stages dismantled language qualifications for matriculation we surrendered a safeguard of academic quality in the University at large. Moreover, our History Faculty, unlike sister departments elsewhere, is not allowed to impose its own linguistic conditions because we must be prepared to let chemists or sociologists read one part of our tripos who are free to come to the study of their other specialism without such compulsion. Pressed for money, the Seeley Historical Library has pretty well ceased to buy books in languages other than English, though admittedly some of the recent work in social history, especially but not only from the United States, in effect demands a knowledge of a difficult variant of the mother tongue. Put a book written in French or German on the shelves, and it will retain its pristine beauty – an untouchable ice princess among the much handled, much defaced crowd of more promiscuous sisters. When recently I included two essays in German in a volume of collected papers – on the grounds that they had been written and published in that language – one reviewer blamed me for not translating them first.

So one of George I's purposes has been ignored by the historians of Cambridge, nor is the existence of a tripos of modern and medieval languages much excuse for that lapse. The other purpose, it seems to me, is in danger of going the same way. True, for a hundred years or so we have been using the study of history for the training of state servants, for the preparation of properly educated minds capable of judging a situation, of assessing human beings, of fitting their actions into traditions so that if change was needed it would at least have a reasonable chance of actually working. We have also kept the study of history alive and flourishing by something that neither George I nor any public figure of his time thought significant – by the practice of fruitful historical research and the training of our successors. This, however, is a theme that I do not propose to discuss today. Nor do I wish to consider the studies which we are increasingly urged to substitute for history in our preparation of public servants and their like. If the time ever comes that we shall be governed by graduates in the social sciences or computer studies or perhaps linguistics, there will be a darkness at noon which will call for the services of the historian to restore the light of day. Historians take long views: we can wait for our return to the favour which for a century landed us with undergraduates of whom many had only a marginal interest in what we were talking about. In any case, for the present the hostile voices, however loud, come from quite a small minority, though it includes men of influence. I see some signs of premature panic among colleagues which I cannot regard as appropriate to the *iucunda gravitas* of our profession. Those hostile voices sound strongest in the lower reaches of our schools, and if this means that more people will escape having all interest in history drummed out of them before they are old enough to like looking at the past, so much the better.

What I want to consider today is one phenomenon which seems to me to lie behind the decline of history as a study for the servants of the state and which has received surprisingly little attention. The modern history we have used in the past to educate our students always included a variety of ages, countries and nations, but it gathered around a central theme, the history of England. In some places it still does, mainly because they do not have experts in Mexico or Malawi to vary the diet drastically. But here it does not, nor does it flourish anywhere any longer with that coherent confidence in an ordered story which made the undergraduate study of history satisfying and the virtues of historical studies immediately apparent, however far removed it might be from the real professional investigation of any part of it. In the last thirty years or so it has, I think, become accepted wisdom that there is a lot of history outside England, a point not unknown to all of us but by some not thought altogether

8

decisive in the construction of courses for study that had to be completed within three years. So by stages all kinds of very interesting topics have been introduced into the tripos for the double purpose of giving a wider experience to undergraduates and a voice to persuasive practitioners of other histories. Nothing, I agree, is wrong with this in principle, but the consequences have been unexpected – not unexpected by all of us – and to some extent disastrous.

Our historical tripos now lacks all cohesion and with it any real understanding of what it is trying to do; the only thing for which it is excellent is the training of that small minority of students who go on to research. In part II, our undergraduates now study a few very very short periods, and if they also offer a dissertation they specialize (allowing for the different length of their studies) quite as much as do research students, whose excessive concentrations on one topic used to be deplored by progressive reformers. Nor does part I offer a real chance to study history in perspective: specialization affects it too. No one reading our subject in this University needs to involve himself in more than about fifty years of English and perhaps a hundred years of European history. Moreover, the options on offer have multiplied so recklessly that one comes to doubt whether any two undergraduates pursue the same course. All very free and generous, and I do not in the least doubt the fascination of many of those options: though I do think it unwise to teach quite so many bits of history in which not enough people have yet worked to provide a solid body of properly criticized sources and writings. This lack tends to reduce the mind-training capacity of historical study. Worse, however, is the fact that in the process one of the chief virtues of that study has vanished as the student is never made to watch developments over a real stretch of time and is not rendered capable of measuring different experiences against each other. We cannot be doing right when we send people into the world who have graduated in history and have never been made to feel the length of it. The current list of part II dissertations leans overwhelmingly towards the last century and a half, with a high proportion of them looking at the 1930s and 1960s. For them the past reaches at best to the day before yesterday, and social studies have crept in by the backdoor. But I do not think that those for whom the past extends from 1066 to perhaps 1350 are any better off.

No one, of course, can study all history; a considerable degree of specialization is bound to prevail. So long as there is one strong element of real continuity in the course, specialization elsewhere does good. In an English University, peopled by undergraduates somewhat averse to reading foreign languages, that element of continuity would naturally be the history of England. But just as that theme became most urgently needed it lost all selfconfidence and joined the rush down the specialist slope – fragmenting into ever smaller pieces, some scintillating like diamonds but others as dull as honest sand. It would seem to be widely held that this is a good thing. A course built around a long stretch of English history is likely to get called chauvinist or ethnocentric, or whatever the latest vogue word of condemnation may be: even perhaps elitist, and you can't say worse than that. It goes against the liberal grain to give the next generation a large dollop of the history of their own country; it goes against the mentality created by genuine research to give the next generation anything not worked down to the roots. Of course, there are other countries and other themes worth getting to know, but why should this mean that English students of history must really be prevented from studying the history of their own nation? I have an advantage here: I cannot be accused of mindless patriotism acquired by the accident of birth. Perhaps one who came to England and English history from outside may be allowed to break a lance for both of them.

Let us therefore now look at the kinds of argument which I have seen or heard advanced against giving English history a dominant role in English historical studies. The chief of them seem to have impressed a lot of people. It maintains that whereas at one time it was possible to tell a tale of coherent development, a tale which made sense, this cannot now be done. It is indeed the case that until, perhaps, the end of the second world war the history of England could with some conviction be construed around a dominant theme. Three such themes stood out any one of which used to serve very well. One was the history of political freedom – the story of constitutional development which tracked the roots of Mr Gladstone's House of Commons to the Anglo-Saxon Witenagemot, or at least to Magna Carta. A second was the growth of empire – the spread of the English over the world. The third, less amenable to such progressive treatment but still capable of accommodating itself to it, looked at England as the mother of industry and wrote the story around the development of trade and manufacture. All three held to a strong theme; all three underwrote notions of progress; all three ended on a high note and could thus serve the cause of self-esteem and selfsatisfaction.

In addition, all three had an inestimable advantage which is too rarely recognized. They all offered a lovely stamping ground to both the admirer and the detractor. This is obviously true of the former, the bard of demi-paradises: by the time you had reached Victoria's empire, governed by an ideal constitutional monarchy through a Parliament which embodied all political wisdom, and fuelled by the ever-expanding wealth produced by science and industry, you hardly needed to explain the central significance of your story – the central significance, that is, which it held for all mankind. In England, at least, the fact that English history most convincingly demonstrated how man should order his existence on earth required no more than an apparently modest rehearsal of what had happened there in the course of a thousand years. But lo and behold: exactly the same story would serve to demon-strate the opposite with equal coherence and conviction. All you had to do was turn the medal over. What I may call the Froude complex – the belief that the blessings of providence have fallen exclusively upon this island – has always been matched by the *New Statesman* complex, the assurance that all things human are absolutely at their worst in this country. Those who praised the unique amalgam represented by a nation united under its rulers stood opposed – indeed, stand opposed – by those who know that structures and consciousness of class are found only in England. Those who looked with starry eyes upon the civilizing mission of anti-slavery frigates and heroic (if rather juvenile) district commissioners faced the determined enemies of colonial exploitation and racial prejudice, so different, they proclaimed, from the welcome extended by France to her overseas territories. (The hallmark of the *New Statesman* complex is the belief that all things French are wonderful.) Encomia on a tolerant and kindly society (remember the unarmed policemen?) had to confront believers in the special depravity of a people of hypocrites, uniquely devoted to what was then called the English vice, whether this meant sexual aberration or oppression of the poor. Only in England, said the one side, was political freedom fully established; only in England, replied the other, was economic freedom systematically suppressed. It was such a lovely medal of which both sides made history so easy. No matter whether you put a plus or a minus sign before your construct, in either way you testified to your belief that England and her history enjoyed the special privilege of providing an example to mankind – an example of either encouragement or warning.

This simple belief has gone, though the plus sign vanished before its counterpart of which, thanks to the continued existence of the *New Statesman*, one can still find fading traces. In consequence, if I understand the argument correctly, it follows that since English history no longer has those lessons to teach there is no reason for presenting it any longer at proper length. What virtue can there be in studying the muddled history of a small offshore island whose supposed achievements have turned out illusory? This abdication from prominence gets justified on one of three grounds, two of which strike me as unconvincing while the third does need serious consideration. Let me dispose of the two which deserve to be called absurd. The empire is gone, we hear, which leaves a small bit of Europe undeserving, in its current political and social confusion, of anybody's serious attention: what right have we to wish to concentrate young minds upon its history? Of course, the empire has gone, not for the first time as it happens, and of course the country is in trouble: but why should this terminate interest in its history? Do not those very facts make that history more interesting and accessible, inasmuch as the subject is in a manner concluded and can be viewed with a hindsight untroubled by the daily addition of new developments? And why should the decline of English, or indeed British, weight in the world affect the case at all? Are we to study only the history of nations that at the moment look like being successful? In 1984, I am not sure that that principle would leave us with any history worth studying. Where is Bohun, where is Bigod, where is Mortimer – all right. Perhaps even where is Lloyd George, where is Winston Churchill, where is Wedgwood Benn. But how do we stand on where is Franklin Delano Roosevelt, where is Vladimir Illyitch Lenin?

I do not seem to have heard similarly humble considerations advanced in other countries that have undergone a decline in power and influence. So the reasons behind this peculiar argument really boil down to the second absurd proposition: since we have lost the sense of superiority that used to sustain us, we can no longer ask anyone – not even English men and women – to concern themselves at length with the history of this country. Sackcloth and ashes, expiating for past arrogance. We have discovered that we have nothing to teach, only to learn, and we thus must send ourselves and our children to school in the history of the United States, of China, above all of that curious extra-terrestrial place known as the Third World. In teaching, though not as yet in research in which reality has a way of shouldering fantasy aside, all things outside Europe are more glamorous than anything European, and within Europe these islands bring up a rear which is best ignored. Those of us who thought that we had succeeded in stemming the tide of Toynbeeism are beginning to realize that we crowed too soon. The extravagances of his bizarre scales of values penetrated more deeply into academic consciousness than I for one had understood.

However, as I have said, I feel myself unusually well qualified to preach against this sort of defeatism. Coming to country and history only in my late teens, I can emphasize to you the special virtues of both without risking charges of inborn chauvinism and narrowness of mind. My experience of other countries stems not from reading about them or visiting them: I have lived in several, and while I lived there had no inkling that I might come to live here. Let me therefore say quite simply this: England is, perhaps was, different from any other country I know at first or second hand. As a society and a body politic it is unique in ways which are exceptionally instructive and, considering the nature of man and of the world he has built for himself, exceptionally consoling. I am not suffering from the Froude complex. I know very well that this is not a realm of unfailing virtue and goodness. That does not alter the fact that it managed to produce a form of existence which is freer of sin against one's neighbour than any other community has attained. I know as well as anyone that its managements, its unions, its weather and its restaurants stand a long way behind qualities easily attained elsewhere. But it excels in having come to terms with the fact that people in large numbers need both to be conscious of one another and leave one another alone. Its people have contributed disproportionately to the stock of human invention and achievement, and they have done so in ways which testify to the differences that make the English so peculiar in the eyes of conventional Europeans. And since it is obviously desirable to understand how an organism so untypical and yet so generally successful actually worked, the history of England retains its special claim to attention.

If I am told that difference and success lie in the past – that England has now abandoned both its singularity and its power to achieve anything – I, who at times find myself leaning to that opinion too, must stress that this makes engagement with the country's history even more important. History is the study of the past; England is past; ergo, we should concentrate upon its history. Perhaps we may pick up some lessons for the present, but in an age which avidly seeks to use history only for this inappropriate and usually misleading purpose we should not trouble ourselves too much about that. No matter what history we study or teach, the generality, led by traitors within the camp, will in any case think that it needs the past only in order to confirm the misguided prejudices and errors by which it orders its present. We cannot prevent this, though we can stop ourselves from pandering to it; and by sticking to history as it was we may even force people to take note of a real rather than a contrived past. However, I commend the study of English history not because it teaches lessons but because it is concerned with a most uncommon phenomenon, so peculiar and special that it can help to correct a great many one-sided views about the past and about mankind. The fact that that history, by the side of a record of folly and horror, tells much that is reassuring about the human animal, its skills and its intelligence and its occasional good sense, is a bonus but it does not constitute the main reason for studying the history of England in a long perspective. That main reason lies in the fact that it offers a singularly helpful way for coming to terms with the past, and a singularly instructive guide to the variety of the past.

In the long perspective: it is here that the third objection, the only one that strikes me as valid, puts in its word. This points out that the proliferation of historical research has made it impossible to contrive any reasonably coherent framework in which a long stretch of English history might be accommodated: everything we say has its exceptions, and there are no great themes left. The progress of knowledge has afflicted English history in two ways. In the first place it has destroyed the comfortable assumptions of the older view which was specifically useful for King George's purpose – the view that one should structure English history around the growth of constitutional freedoms and especially the history of Parliament. Secondly, it looks as though there is now so much particular history about – such various and often contested details to take into account – that it is futile even to attempt to pull our understanding into a story which can cover more than a few decades – a century at most, and even that is difficult.

Having spent most of my career in denouncing and demolishing received wisdom, I am very conscious of the fact that a long-lived and comprehensible story lies broken in pieces around us and cannot possibly be resuscitated. A few quite cuddly survivors from before the Flood – antediluvians indeed – still chunter on, mostly in the United States, emitting smoke signals which speak of the growth of liberty, the role of a freedom-guarding Parliament, the wonders of democracy, but I can see no virtue in telling a tale of demonstrable error for the sake of bringing English history to our students, or indeed to anyone else. No: the Stubbs–Pollard–Neale–Notestein–Morley–Arthur Bryant tradition is dead and should remain decently buried: the whigs have had their day.

It was not Butterfield who did for the whigs: the Indian sign has been on them ever since Maitland, in his modestly apologetic fashion, threw his bomb about the Parliament of 1305 into the ring, a bomb fitted with so slow a fuse that it took decades to explode properly. It may not now be recalled what resistance and contumely H. G. Richardson and George Sayles encountered when they took Maitland seriously and rewrote the history of the medieval Parliament by telling what have now become the commonplaces of our understanding. Perhaps they did not improve their chances of acceptance by the severity of their language, but the resistance was emotional and based on a liberal consensus. Oxford in particular would not surrender Stubbs, but Helen Cam, at some other place, also tried to save him. I am reminded of the misplaced zeal with which at this time so many historians, alleged revisionists among them, tell us that S. R. Gardiner never erred. In a way, there is a special appropriateness in the accident that the demolition charge was laid by one who thought himself a lawyer. For this teleological history, which followed the rise of Parliament and freedom and which so powerfully attracted especially

American historians, was really put together by lawyers who first organized it in the seventeenth century (re-placing the sixteenth century's preoccupation with dyn-asties) and then imposed it with all the authority of the law. What a time it has taken us to shake off the shackles of the law – to make a reality of that emancipation of history from the lawyers which the separate creation of an his-torical tripos attempted to symbolize in 1875! However, we have our compensations. At long last Maitland's gen-eral guidance is being heeded and legal historians write historians', not lawyers', history. True, they tend to bewilder some lawyers, but (as they know very well) the guest bedrooms are being got ready in the mansion of history.

The abandoning of false trails should only lead to a search for more reliable roads. Here, however, the explorer does meet the real problems raised by the con-stant progress of research. Whatever may today be true of British manufacturing industry, the productivity of the scholarly sector is awesome. The *Annual Bibliography* which I edit has now covered nine years, in which time we have added well over 25,000 items to the study of British and Irish history: and I cannot even claim absolutely total coverage. Not all those pieces, of course, are important, but some that do not themselves add to knowledge even more menacingly provide access to yet more new sources for it. New journals seem to appear every year: the last three years have witnessed the arrival of two concerned with representative institutions and three inviting discus-sions of the law and its social function. Old journals have grown at a rate of almost Israelian inflation. In 1958, when we dropped the prefix 'Cambridge' from the *Historical*

Journal, the first volume ran to 207 pages; a quarter century later, volume 25 used up 1038. Not all this material pertains to English history, but a great deal does. There is assuredly an awful lot more of it to accommodate in the story, if ever it will actually be told, than faced the scholar just one generation ago.

A mere recital of bulk does not fully describe the problem. Much of that new history has been added outside the trusty old compartments of politics, administration, war and peace, though some of it – especially some endeavours in the history of the mind and of the fine arts – will cause no difficulties in the taking on of long stretches of English history. On the other hand, much social history will have to be incorporated: even plain economic history has been giving way to various forms of social studies. I will silence my doubts about much of that work on children, women and marriage; sometimes it does not seem overwhelmingly central to one's concerns. To cite two real and recent examples: will it matter to a history of England that someone has spent time on 'Single women in the London marriage market: age, status and mobility 1598–1619', and someone else on 'The regulation of sexuality since 1800'? Much social history has a charming quality of timelessness: the facts of birth, copulation and death do not alter all that much through the ages – not nearly so much as some historians would like to believe. On the other hand, the study of crime or trades unions (the juxtaposition reveals my unconscious) does very definitely affect the way we look upon and understand the past, as do novel findings on peasant landholding in the thirteenth century or analyses of the distribution of wealth in the nineteeth. Much of this history, we should remember, will turn out to be provisional and even ephemeral. In the history of crime, for instance, at present a very popular genre, too much work tends to be weak on the law and strong on the author's social convictions: too often we meet there unhistorical purposes behind the work and somewhat dubious methods which suggest that we shall have to jettison ballast as well as acquire knowledge as we absorb the progress of research.

Revisionism is going on along the whole front of English history, and rightly so; but while some of it has already irremediably transformed many sectors, I rather think that a notable part of this new history will turn out to stand in need of revision itself, quite often back to square one. Not all exploded history will stay as dead as the parliamentary and puritan oppositions to Elizabeth I. An odd thing has happened to the poor of Elizabethan England, always known to be burdened with hard and horrid lives. However, we used to think that they were probably better off than their predecessors: there seemed to be signs to that effect. Of late, on the other hand, the period has been getting itself pigeonholed under the slogan 'pauperization of the poor' – a conviction that they were declining from a barely tolerable into a totally intolerable condition. These pauperized poor were bred out of mathematics, namely the discrepancy between the fast rise of prices and the slow rise of wages, rather than out of positive evidence. For some historians their existence survived the curious absence of the sort of consequences one would have expected to show up, such as famine, food riots, subsistence crises – all quite well vouched for in other countries. They survived the uncomfortable demonstration of quite positive improvements in the food supply. At this moment, however, they look like once again vanishing into the woodwork before a dawning suspicion that the apparently reliable calculation of wage rates does not accurately reflect the means of livelihood available to the lower orders of Elizabethan England. Shortly, I think, we shall not be forced to incorporate an element of major economic decline in a picture which also includes the great rebuilding of England and the signs of augmenting wealth well down the scale found in inventories and wills. Quite a few such seemingly awkward novelties may well disappear under further scrutiny: after all, historical knowledge rightly progresses as a rule in a dialectic of new notions and their limitations. The difficulty lies in knowing where to accept and where to doubt – and to do so without allowing the choice to be ruled by personal prejudice. But at any rate, while trying to keep up we also have to guard against a common and very understandable form of influenza: belief in the latest article.

However, when everything has been done to reduce the flood of innovation to a manageable size of reasonably reliable residues, one problem will remain to hamper the restoration of long stretches of English history to the place they ought to occupy in learning and in teaching. The present predilection for social and intellectual history operates against narrative, against the concept of a moving river of history. It studies the static elements in the stream – the boulders, the jammed tree-trunks, at best the eddies. Social analysis works by tactics which bring the stream to a halt, and it studies cross-sections. The French preceptors who prescribe these exercises have told us that they wish to make history stand still so that it can be analysed. I

22

will not today contemplate any further this, to me, very odd endeavour which seems to suppose that history can be studied only by perverting its fundamental nature. But I draw your attention to the inadequacy of any historical analysis which is not predominantly directed towards an understanding of change through time. The present flood of historians' labours includes a great many contributions which not only, and quite rightly, study particular problems hard to incorporate in a story, but by the methods they favour positively inhibit our grasp of movement and transformation. I might add that by the language which so many of them employ they inhibit interest in history altogether. A history simply is not equal to a collection or even a sequence of technically analysed sociological states.

To sum up: any effort to seek a proper understanding of this country's past over some ten centuries faces present convictions which declare that such ambitions are intellectually mistaken and also irrelevant or even immoral in a world in which England no longer plays a major or exemplary role. Against this I set two counter-claims.

In the first place, the new history now produced must demand to be turned to historical purposes. The people who so diligently and often productively study it call it history; and they are right in this even when they fail to notice how their own methods stand in the way of truly historical thinking about the past. The undoubted fact that it has become very difficult to write a history even of one century which is not hopelessly out of date on detail or superficial in its main concerns presents no reason whatsoever for abandoning the task. Since unquestionably the people who lived through the experiences analysed by the historians of social structure, economic function, changing views on religion or magic, did live in England at identifiable points in time, it must be the task of the historian to incorporate the new knowledge in the older practice of continuous history. And in the second place I repeat what I said before. The long-term history of England continues to merit attention even though the empire is gone and we no longer wish to show off the Westminster Parliament as the last word in political wisdom. Without being in the least committed to a narrow and bigoted patriotism or blind to a wider world, one may still claim on good grounds, as I do, that special interest and importance attaches to the history of a country whose past achievements were so formidable and influential – a country whose social, legal and political machineries differed so noticeably and so influentially from the practices of all other countries. It is right that the history of the rest of the world should be diligently studied and that some acquaintance with it should be brought to English students. But I am willing to maintain that we shall never properly understand the history of the last millennium unless we preserve and improve our understanding of the way in which over that long span of time the people and rulers of England – for most of that time a small and seemingly insignificant realm – managed their existence between those two inescapable reference points: the misery of birth and the certainty of death. And if we wish to understand this we shall have to study them in a continuum, not in portions or sections.

High claims, no doubt, and easy to assert, but can it not be done? If we can no longer fall back on a history of political progress, how shall we write the history of England? I can think of one or two themes, continuous or recurrent, around which it might be constructed, but I realize that to the demographer, the analyst and the specialist in the twentieth century they will probably appear superficial, even frivolous. (Not that frivolity should be deplored: one thing I have against the analysts is the deadly seriousness they apply to everything.) What other nation has gained and lost so many empires? Counting the Plantagenet effort, I make it three: perhaps there are more. What nation has more regularly recruited itself from other people and submerged their distinguishing characteristics – including the Welsh and Scottish neighbours? It is engaged in doing so once more today. It would be possible to write a good history of England around her relations with the continent or around her peculiar law. These approximate suggestions all share the three essential ingredients: they are interesting in themselves; their proper understanding calls for a very extended time-span; and they emphasize the difference that is England. So, I admit, would a history of England written round the game of cricket – and what monumentally tedious studies of social structure that would bring in!

I should, however, quite seriously draw attention to one element of continuity which is too rarely noticed. Until very recently, the minds and attitudes of the English people were ruled by two attempts to provide anchor-points of moderate certainty in a manifestly uncertain and dangerous world. The instruments were religion (reassurance in the hereafter) and law (reassurance down here). Not everybody shared identical views of either, and both changed a great deal in the course of history: but they were always there, to frame the way in which people regarded their existence. I feel a certain duty incumbent upon me to call attention to these fundamental embodiments of change and continuity because I happen at present to be president of both the Ecclesiastical History Society and the Selden Society – an engrossment of offices which makes me feel much more sympathetic towards Cardinal Wolsey. The experience has made me realize more than ever I did before how central to the continuous history of England are religion in one form or other and law in one application or other – and how useful they both therefore become in the writing of that continuous history on terms which the depth of modern research demands. I really think that they will serve much better than the ups and downs of social mobility or the export trade: but they will be much harder to manage properly.

If today we wish to grasp English history in the round, we seek a history which remembers the existence of the people who, in Thomas Smith's words, do not hold rule, and the fact of the shires and boroughs away from the centre. It must be the history of a whole society in active operation. I will confess to my preferred theme which will surprise no one but which is chosen because it would, I think, still make it possible to tie the detail on a continuous thread and embrace just about every aspect of this society without false artifice. That theme is government and politics – the manner in which this society managed to civilize power and order itself through constant changes. It is a history which cannot be properly written without regard for those continuous influences on the public and the private mind – religion and the law. It must attend to movement and change, escaping the falsely static impressions that would be left by a story built round strictly social and economic history which yet it cannot do without. A main thread spun out of the history of royal government and the law would necessarily incorporate the strands of particularity and localism; it would much more correctly present the growth of that peculiar English mixture of order and disorder, control and freedom, than would the traditional tale of Parliament; and it would be forced to remember all the people – governors as well as governed, clergy as well as laity, thieves as well as hangmen, husbandmen as well as philosophers, philistines as well as poets. Not to mention women as well as men. And since the prime interest of royal government has always looked to relations with other realms it would inevitably place England within the larger world, thus avoiding the dangers of insularity.

It is easy, or relatively easy, to list such notions; writing the story is another matter. After what I said about Acton's inaugural lecture, I ought to be more careful: I should not pretend to a skill I do not have. But remember that my starting point was the history we teach, not the history we write; and when we teach we do not expect to get everything in that should be in, nor do we expect one man to cover all the ground. But we do not teach well unless we compel attention to long stretches of English history. It is, I maintain, still as possible as it is necessary to allow the history of England to form the backbone of that awareness of the past which it is our duty to awake and maintain in others as well as ourselves.

For let us not underestimate the task we face. I have today been speaking in the main about the teaching of history, especially at the Universities, but I think we need to consider much larger issues – issues larger than the possible end to the employment of history graduates in schools. An age of uncertainty, beset by false faiths and the prophets of constant innovation, badly needs to know its roots. Yet it is one of the peculiarities of English society – one of the ways in which it differs so much from other societies known to me – that it largely lacks an active sense of history. The many people who confuse conservatism and pageantry with a sense of history will find this hard to believe, but it is a serious truth about the English in the mass that they know very little and care not greatly about their history. The past really does not sit upon their backs, burdening the present: and if you doubt this, I ask you to consider the Irish or the Scots, the Germans or the Russians, not to mention the French (certain that no other people has a history worth the name) who have never ceased to behave as though Louis XIV or Napoleon was still around. This quality of English life has notable attractions. Because we in this country forget the past almost as soon as it has become the past, we do not need for ever to expiate it, avenge it, kiss its dead hand. But that quality has equally notable drawbacks. When a past is wanted for present uses, whether by way of reassurances or for the justification of some new and drastic action, it is not the real past that is wheeled into line but one constructed by partisans for the use of the moment. The use of the moment has its claims and can sometimes justly be responsible for which part of the past gets emphasized. Ages dominated by the Froude complex have needed the deflationary effects of a history recording misdeeds and miseries. A *New Statesman* era like ours, full of self-deprecation and envy, can do with the corrective of a past that demonstrates virtue and achievement. But we, as historians, do not write history for the use of the moment;

we are the guardians and the distributors of the truths of history and should at least try to make sure than when current partisans plunder history for their own purposes they have a non-partisan and real history to stand over them. We neglect a duty if we do not treat the history of this country as a continuum worthy of discovery and a story worthy to be told.

The apprehensions which caused King George I to found this Regius chair are not absent from our lives. He, or his advisers, thought that a University curriculum dominated by the arid scholarship of classical learning failed to offer the nation that understanding of itself without which it could not hope to maintain and improve itself. Not all our current studies are as arid, or indeed as scholarly, as the humanities threatened to be in the age of Bentley. However, danger cones are flying. As the social scientists – a contradiction in terms – build their ahistorical models of a society that this or that operator would like to set up, to fulfil purposes which range from the fantasies of the unbalanced to the ignorant compassions of the uninstructed, the possibility grows rapidly that the problems we confront will be solved in ways totally destructive of what made England a country worth living in – a country worth coming to. I have said it before but it cannot be said often enough: it is one of the functions of the historian to prevent such disasters by telling the truth about the past without having it in mind to call up the past to come to the rescue of the present. Only if he avoids the temptations of devising comfortable theories and allegedly usable laws of human behaviour, only if he rejects all pontificating that puts the past tendentiously at the service of the present, will he in fact discharge his duty to that present. He serves best when he demonstrates the variety and unpredictability of the past and remembers all the world of humanity. There was a time when historians and teachers of history, conscious of insularity, rightly went forth to fetch home all the tea in China and all the quinine in Peru. Those harvests are gathered in and insularity is distant. Today, I hope, some of us will come back home and think home good enough to tell its long story to the world.